Trout Are Made of Trees

April Pulley Sayre

Illustrated by Kate Endle

 Charlesbridge

For Tom and Veda, who appreciate
the connections—A. P. S.

Acknowledgments:

Thank you to fact checker/seeker Jeff Sayre, aquatic ecologist
Dr. Gary Lamberti of Notre Dame, Warren Colyer of Trout
Unlimited, Nathan Bridges, and Mary Lee Hahn.—A. P. S.

Special thanks to Chris Harvey for his research efforts.
Thanks, also, to Susan Sherman and Emily Mitchell for
their interest and efforts.—K. E.

Published by Charlesbridge
85 Main Street
Watertown, MA 02472
(617) 926-0329
www.charlesbridge.com

Library of Congress Cataloging-in-Publication Data
Sayre, April Pulley.
    Trout are made of trees / April Pulley Sayre; illustrated by Kate Endle.
        p. cm.
    ISBN 978-1-58089-137-0 (reinforced for library use)
    ISBN 978-1-58089-138-7 (softcover)
1. Stream ecology—Juvenile literature. 2. Food chains (Ecology)—Juvenile literature.
I. Endle, Kate, ill. II. Title.
QH541.5.S7S29 2008
577′.16—dc22   2007002268

Printed in China
(hc) 10 9 8 7 6 5 4 3 2
(sc) 10 9 8 7 6 5 4 3 2

Illustrations created with mixed media collage and adhered to
    300-lb. Arches cold-press watercolor paper
Display type and text type set in Billy, a SparkyType family member,
    designed by David "Sparky" Buck
Color separations by Chroma Graphics, Singapore
Printed and bound by Everbest Printing Company, Ltd.,
    through Four Colour Imports, Ltd., Louisville, Kentucky
        Production supervision by Brian G. Walker

Trout are made of trees.

In fall, trees let go of leaves,
which swirl and twirl
and slip into streams.

They ride in a rush
above rocks
and over rapids.

They snag and settle soggily down.

Bacteria feed on the leaves.

Algae grow, softening surfaces.

Next the shredders move in:
Crane flies, caddisflies,
shrimp, and stoneflies shred leaves.
Rip and snip!
They eat the algae-covered leaves,
which become part of them.

Meanwhile predators are swimming and stalking. . . .
Crunch—there go the caddisflies!

Munch—there go the stoneflies!

Now the leaves have become part of the predators.

Trout join in. Swim and snap!
Fins flick. Rush. Zap!

They eat dragonflies, caddisflies, stoneflies, and minnows.

The leaves have now become part of the trout.

Tree shade keeps the stream cool for spawning.

Female trout gather over gravel and lay eggs.

The males fertilize the eggs.

Here come the hatchlings!

They grow up in a stream
—Crack! Kersplash!—
shaped by fallen branches.

Trout are made of trees.

So are the bears

and the people

who catch the trout and eat them.

The Trout Life Cycle

Trout are one part of a vast food web centered in streams and rivers. Trout require cool, clean water to survive. Trees shade streams, helping keep the water cool. As streamwater winds its way past fallen branches and rocks, it speeds up in some places and slows down in others. Fast-flowing water scours away dirt, leaving gravel. This creates the perfect nesting place for trout.

Fanning her tail and fins, a female trout sweeps away the top layer of gravel to create a pit—the nest. She lays several thousand eggs in the nest. A male trout swims over the nest and fertilizes the eggs. The male and female cover the eggs with gravel, then leave.

In about a month, the eggs hatch. Each young trout, called an alevin, has a yolk sac attached to its body. This sac provides nutrients. Once the sac is used up and absorbed into its body, the alevin swims out of the gravel. At this stage young trout are called fry.

Fry hide in quiet pools, among tree roots and branches that have fallen into the water. They eat aquatic insects—insects that live in the water—as well as tiny crustaceans and plankton. Many of these creatures feed on leaves that fall into the stream. As the trout grow they also feed on larger animals such as snails, small fish, tadpoles, and adult frogs. When trout mature they spawn, or mate, and produce a new generation of trout. These trout, like their parents, feed on the insects who feed on the leaves that fall from the trees near the stream.

Be a Stream Hero!

- Encourage landowners to leave plants at the edges of streams and lakes. They should not mow right to the edge of a stream or allow cows, goats, or horses to graze too close to the water. Tall plants at the edges of streams help cool a stream and protect its banks. Dragonflies, frogs, and other creatures need these stream and river edges, called riparian areas, as habitat.

- Never pour paint, oil, or other dangerous chemicals into the storm drains on streets. Encourage landowners to avoid using pesticides and fertilizers on lawns near streams. These chemicals can run into streams and pollute them.

- Adopt a stream! Join with local organizations for streambank cleanup days. Learn how to test the water in local streams for pollution, and how to survey the stream for aquatic insects.

Resources for Further Information

American Rivers • www.americanrivers.org
Learn about endangered rivers, endangered species, and how you can help conserve these natural resources.

Chesapeake Bay Foundation • www.cbf.org
Save the Bay! Discover how to protect and preserve the Chesapeake Bay through CBF's environmental education program.

Moyle, Peter B. *Fish: An Enthusiast's Guide.* Berkeley, CA: University of California Press, 1993.

Page, Lawrence M. and Burr, Brooks M. *A Field Guide to Freshwater Fishes: North America North of Mexico.* Peterson Field Guides. Boston: Houghton Mifflin, 1991.

Project Wet! Water Education for Teachers • www.projectwet.org
Learn about rivers, streams, fish, and wetlands, with lessons and activities you can do with your class.

River Network • www.rivernetwork.org
Find out how to make a difference in the quality of our rivers and the water we drink, with easy actions you can take at home.

Sayre, April Pulley. *River and Stream.* New York: Twenty-First Century Books, 1996.

Sayre, April Pulley. *Trout, Trout, Trout: A Fish Chant.* Chanhassen, MN: NorthWord Press, 2004.

Smith, C. Lavett. *Fish Watching: An Outdoor Guide to Freshwater Fishes.* Ithaca, NY: Comstock Publishing, 1994.

Trout Unlimited • www.tu.org
Help protect trout habitats by supporting this grassroots advocacy group.